# POKE CAKES
## AND MORE!

D1406977

Publications International, Ltd.

**Microwave Cooking:** Microwave ovens vary in wattage. Use the cooking times as guidelines and check for doneness before adding more time.

# TABLE OF
# Contents

# POKE CAKES

# RED, WHITE AND BLUE POKE CAKE

1 package (about 15 ounces) white cake mix, plus ingredients to prepare mix

2 cups boiling water, divided

1 package (4-serving size) cherry gelatin

1 package (4-serving size) blue-raspberry gelatin

2 packages (8 ounces each) cream cheese

2 jars (7 ounces each) marshmallow creme

2 teaspoons vanilla

1. Preheat oven to 350°F. Grease and flour two 9-inch round cake pans.

2. Prepare cake mix according to package directions. Pour batter evenly into prepared pans. Bake 25 minutes or until toothpick inserted into centers comes out clean. Cool completely in pans on wire rack.

3. Combine 1 cup boiling water and cherry gelatin in small bowl; stir until gelatin is completely dissolved. Combine remaining 1 cup boiling water and blue-raspberry gelatin in separate small bowl; stir until gelatin is completely dissolved. Pour red gelatin over one cake layer and blue gelatin over the other cake layer. Refrigerate 3 hours.

4. Meanwhile, combine cream cheese, marshmallow creme and vanilla in medium bowl with electric mixer at medium-high speed until smooth and fluffy.

5. Unmold one cake layer onto large serving plate. Spread with about 1 cup frosting. Unmold second cake layer; carefully place on first cake layer. Frost top and sides of cake with remaining frosting. Refrigerate 1 hour or until ready to serve. Store any leftover cake in refrigerator.

*Makes 10 to 12 servings*

# POKED S'MORES CAKE

1 package (about 15 ounces) chocolate cake mix, plus ingredients to prepare mix

½ (7-ounce) jar marshmallow creme

¾ cup plus 1 tablespoon whipping cream, divided

2 cups semisweet chocolate chips

1 cup graham cracker crumbs

1. Prepare and bake cake mix according to package directions for 13×9-inch pan. Cool completely.

2. Microwave marshmallow creme with 1 tablespoon whipping cream in small microwave-safe bowl on HIGH 30 seconds; stir until smooth. Poke holes in cake at 1-inch intervals with round wooden spoon handle. Pour marshmallow mixture over cake.

3. Combine 1 cup chocolate chips and remaining ¾ cup whipping cream in medium saucepan. Cook and stir over medium heat until chocolate is half melted. Remove from heat. Add remaining 1 cup chocolate chips; stir until smooth. Pour melted chocolate over cake. Refrigerate 2 to 3 hours or until firm.

4. Top with graham cracker crumbs just before serving.

*Makes 12 to 15 servings*

# PEANUT BUTTER AND JELLY POKE CAKE

1 pound cake (14 to 16 ounces), thawed if frozen

½ cup plus 2 tablespoons strawberry jam, divided

1 to 2 tablespoons water

½ cup (1 stick) butter, softened

½ cup creamy peanut butter

2 cups powdered sugar

2 tablespoons milk

¼ teaspoon salt (optional)

1. Poke holes in cake at ½-inch intervals with plastic drinking straw.

2. Melt ½ cup jam with water in small saucepan over low heat, stirring constantly.

3. Spread jam over cake, dripping some jam into holes. Poke holes with toothpick to pop any air bubbles, if necessary. Refrigerate 1 hour or until jam has set.

4. Beat butter and peanut butter in large bowl with electric mixer at medium-high speed until smooth. Add powdered sugar and milk; beat at low speed until blended. Add salt, if desired. Beat at medium-high speed 5 minutes or until very fluffy.

5. Split cake in half crosswise. Spread remaining 2 tablespoons jam over bottom; top with one fourth of frosting. Replace top of cake; frost top with remaining frosting.

*Makes 8 servings*

# Red Velvet Bundt Poke Cake

1 package (about 15 ounces) red velvet cake mix, plus ingredients to prepare mix

1½ cups white chocolate chips, divided

6 tablespoons whipping cream

1. Prepare and bake cake mix according to package directions for bundt pan. Cool completely.

2. Poke holes in cake at ½-inch intervals with wooden skewer. Combine 1 cup white chocolate chips and whipping cream in medium saucepan. Cook and stir over medium heat until chocolate is half melted. Remove from heat. Add remaining ½ cup chocolate chips; stir until smooth. Pour half of melted chocolate into holes of cake. Refrigerate 30 minutes or until set.

3. Unmold cake. Rewarm remaining chocolate; drizzle over cake. Refrigerate 2 to 3 hours or until firm.

*Makes 16 servings*

# CHERRY SODA POKE CAKE

1 package (about 15 ounces) white cake mix, plus ingredients to prepare mix

1 package (4-serving size) cherry gelatin

¾ cup boiling water

½ cup cherry-flavored cola

1 container (8 ounces) frozen whipped topping, thawed

3 tablespoons maraschino cherry juice (optional)

½ cup maraschino cherries

1. Prepare and bake cake according to package directions for 13×9-inch baking pan. Cool completely.

2. Poke holes in cake at ½-inch intervals with round wooden spoon handle. Combine gelatin and boiling water in small bowl; stir until gelatin is dissolved. Add ice to cola to measure 1¼ cups; stir into gelatin mixture. Chill gelatin 15 minutes.

3. Stir gelatin; pour over cake. Combine whipped topping and cherry juice, if desired, in medium bowl. Spread whipped topping on cake; top with cherries. Refrigerate 2 to 3 hours or until firm.

*Makes 12 to 15 servings*

# Rainbow Poke Cake

1 package (about 15 ounces) white cake mix, plus ingredients to prepare mix

Gel food coloring (6 colors)

1 package (4-serving size) orange gelatin

1 cup boiling water

½ cup cold water

1 container (8 ounces) frozen whipped topping, thawed

½ cup colored nonpareils

1. Prepare cake mix according to package directions. Divide batter evenly into six small bowls. Add one food coloring to each individual bowl until desired shade is reached.

2. Prop one end of 13×9-inch pan on wooden spoon; alternately pour batters in crosswise lines into pan. Bake according to package directions; cool completely.

3. Poke holes in cake at ½-inch intervals with fork. Combine gelatin and boiling water in small bowl; stir until gelatin is dissolved. Stir in cold water; cool gelatin slightly. Pour gelatin over cake. Top cake with whipped topping and nonpareils.

*Makes 12 to 15 servings*

# PUMPKIN POKE CAKE

1 package (about 15 ounces) yellow cake mix, plus ingredients to prepare mix

1 can (15 ounces) pumpkin purée

1 can (14 ounces) sweetened condensed milk

2 teaspoons ground cinnamon

1 container (8 ounces) frozen whipped topping, thawed

2 cups chopped toffee bits

1 jar (12 ounces) caramel ice cream topping

1. Prepare and bake cake mix according to package directions for 13×9-inch pan. Cool completely.

2. Poke holes in cake at ½-inch intervals with wooden skewer. Combine pumpkin, sweetened condensed milk and cinnamon in medium bowl; stir until well blended. Pour over cake. Top cake with whipped topping and toffee bits. Refrigerate 2 to 3 hours or until firm. Drizzle with caramel just before serving.

*Makes 12 to 15 servings*

# Lemon Blueberry Poke Bundt Cake

1 package (about 15 ounces) lemon cake mix, plus ingredients to prepare mix

1 can (12 ounces) blueberry pie filling

2 cups powdered sugar

6 to 9 tablespoons whipping cream, divided

1. Prepare and bake cake mix according to package directions in bundt pan. Cool completely.

2. Poke cake at ½-inch intervals with round wooden spoon handle.* Pour blueberry filling over cake. Refrigerate 2 to 3 hours or until firm.

3. Unmold cake onto large serving platter. Combine powdered sugar and 6 tablespoons whipping cream in medium bowl; whisk until smooth. Add enough remaining whipping cream, 1 tablespoon at a time, to make pourable glaze. Pour glaze over cake.

*Makes 16 servings*

*Be sure to move the wooden spoon handle in small circles within each hole before removing it. This will make the holes a bit larger to help the blueberry pieces in the pie filling fit into them.

# GERMAN CHOCOLATE POKE CAKE

1 package (about 15 ounces)
German chocolate cake
mix, plus ingredients to
prepare mix

1 jar (12 ounces) caramel
ice cream topping

1 can (12 ounces)
evaporated milk

¾ cup granulated sugar

¾ cup packed brown sugar

½ cup (1 stick) butter,
softened

4 egg yolks, beaten

2 cups shredded coconut

1 cup chopped pecans

1. Prepare and bake cake mix according to package directions for 13×9-inch pan. Cool completely.

2. Poke holes in cake at ½-inch intervals with wooden skewer. Microwave caramel in jar without lid on HIGH 1 to 2 minutes or until softened; stir. Pour over cake.

3. Combine evaporated milk, granulated sugar, brown sugar, butter and egg yolks in medium saucepan; cook and stir over medium-low heat 8 to 10 minutes or until slightly thickened and mixture just begins to bubble. Stir in coconut and pecans. Remove from heat. Pour coconut mixture over cake. Refrigerate 2 to 3 hours or until firm.

*Makes 12 to 15 servings*

# KEY LIME POKE CAKE

1 package (about 15 ounces) white cake mix, plus ingredients to prepare mix

1 package (4-serving size) lime gelatin, plus water to prepare mix

1 package (8 ounces) cream cheese, softened

1 container (8 ounces) frozen whipped topping, thawed and divided

3 tablespoons milk

2 cups graham cracker crumbs

Lime slices (optional)

1. Prepare and bake cake mix according to package directions for 13×9-inch baking pan. Cool completely.

2. Prepare gelatin according to package directions. Poke holes in cake at ½-inch intervals with round wooden spoon handle. Beat prepared gelatin, cream cheese, ¾ cup whipped topping and milk in large bowl with electric mixer at medium speed until smooth. Spread cream cheese mixture over cake, pushing gently into holes. Top cake with remaining whipped topping. Refrigerate 2 to 3 hours or until firm.

3. Top with graham cracker crumbs just before serving. Garnish with limes.

*Makes 12 to 15 servings*

# MINT-FILLED COOKIES AND CREAM POKE CAKE

1 package (about 15 ounces) white cake mix, plus ingredients to prepare mix

20 chocolate creme-filled sandwich cookies, crushed

1 package (about 3 ounces) instant white chocolate pudding and pie filling mix

2 cups milk

1 teaspoon mint extract

Green food coloring

¾ cup whipping cream

1 cup semisweet chocolate chips

Sprigs fresh mint (optional)

1. Preheat oven to 350°F. Grease and flour two 9-inch round cake pans.

2. Prepare cake mix according to package directions; stir in cookies. Pour batter into prepared pans. Bake 25 minutes or until toothpick inserted into centers comes out clean. Cool completely in pans on wire rack.

3. Loosen cakes from sides and bottoms of pans with knife, thin spatula or fingers. Poke holes all over cakes with round wooden spoon handle.

4. Whisk pudding mix, milk, mint extract and food coloring in large bowl 2 minutes. Spread over cakes. Refrigerate 2 hours.

5. Turn out one cake onto second cake in pan; turn out stack of cakes onto serving plate.

6. Heat whipping cream in small saucepan until bubbles form around edge. Remove from heat. Add chips; whisk until smooth. Pour over cake; spread evenly over top and sides. Refrigerate 1 hour or until topping is set. Garnish with mint sprigs.

*Makes 10 to 12 servings*

# Strawberry Poke Cake

1 package (about 15 ounces) white cake mix, plus ingredients to prepare mix

2 packages (4-serving size each) strawberry gelatin, plus ingredients to prepare mix

1 container (8 ounces) frozen whipped topping, thawed

1 cup sliced fresh strawberries

1. Prepare and bake cake mix according to package directions for 13×9-inch pan. Cool completely.

2. Prepare gelatin according to package directions for quick set method in two separate medium bowls; chill 15 minutes. Poke holes in cake at ½-inch intervals with round wooden spoon handle. Stir one bowl of gelatin; pour over cake. Reserve remaining bowl. Refrigerate cake 1 hour.

3. Stir remaining gelatin; pour over cake top. Top with whipped topping and strawberries. Refrigerate 2 to 3 hours or until firm.

*Makes 12 to 15 servings*

# DUMP CAKES

# S'MORES DUMP CAKE

1 package (about 15 ounces) milk chocolate cake mix

1 package (4-serving size) chocolate instant pudding and pie filling mix

1½ cups milk

1 cup mini marshmallows

3 bars (1.55 ounces each) milk chocolate bars, broken into pieces *or* 1 cup milk chocolate chips

3 whole graham crackers, broken into ½-inch pieces

1. Preheat oven to 350°F. Spray 13×9-inch baking pan with nonstick cooking spray.

2. Combine cake mix, pudding mix and milk in large bowl; beat 1 to 2 minutes or until well blended. Spread evenly in prepared pan.

3. Bake 30 to 35 minutes or until toothpick inserted into center comes out clean. *Turn oven to broil.*

4. Sprinkle marshmallows, chocolate and graham crackers over cake. Broil 6 inches from heat source 30 seconds to 1 minute or until marshmallows are golden brown. (Watch carefully to prevent burning.) Cool at least 5 minutes before serving.

*Makes 12 to 15 servings*

# CHERRY CHEESECAKE DUMP CAKE

1 can (21 ounces) cherry pie filling

1 can (14½ ounces) tart cherries in water, drained

4 ounces cream cheese, cut into small pieces

1 package (about 15 ounces) yellow cake mix

½ cup (1 stick) butter, cut into thin slices

1. Preheat oven to 350°F. Spray 13×9-inch baking pan with nonstick cooking spray.

2. Spread cherry pie filling and cherries in prepared pan. Sprinkle cream cheese pieces over cherries. Top evenly with cake mix. Top with butter in single layer, covering cake mix as much as possible.

3. Bake 45 to 50 minutes or until toothpick inserted into center of cake comes out clean. Cool at least 15 minutes before serving.

*Makes 12 to 15 servings*

# Apricot Double Chip Dump Cake

2 cups apricot preserves
  or jam

½ cup semisweet chocolate
  chips

½ cup white chocolate chips

1 package (about 15 ounces)
  yellow cake mix

½ cup (1 stick) butter, cut
  into thin slices

⅓ cup water

1. Preheat oven to 350°F. Spray 9-inch square baking pan with nonstick cooking spray.

2. Spread preserves in prepared pan. Sprinkle with half of semisweet chips and half of white chips. Top evenly with cake mix. Top with butter in single layer, covering cake mix as much as possible. Drizzle water over top. Sprinkle with remaining semisweet and white chips.

3. Bake 50 to 55 minutes or until toothpick inserted into center comes out clean. Cool at least 15 minutes before serving.

*Makes 9 servings*

# DOUBLE BANANA DUMP CAKE

1 package (about 18 ounces) banana cake mix, plus ingredients to prepare mix

¾ cup chopped hazelnuts or sliced almonds, toasted* and divided

1 banana, thinly sliced

4 tablespoons chocolate hazelnut spread, heated**

*To toast hazelnuts, spread in single layer on ungreased baking sheet. Bake in preheated 350°F oven 5 to 7 minutes or until light brown, stirring occasionally.

**Microwave on LOW (30%) about 1 minute or until pourable.

1. Preheat oven to 350°F. Spray 9-inch square baking pan with nonstick cooking spray.

2. Prepare cake mix according to package directions; stir in ½ cup hazelnuts. Spread half of batter in prepared pan. Top with banana slices; drizzle with 2 tablespoons chocolate hazelnut spread. Top with remaining half of batter; sprinkle with remaining ¼ cup hazelnuts and drizzle with remaining 2 tablespoons chocolate hazelnut spread.

3. Bake 25 to 30 minutes or until toothpick inserted into center comes out clean. Cool in pan 15 minutes before serving.

*Makes 9 servings*

# PINEAPPLE ANGEL DUMP CAKE

2½ cups fresh or thawed frozen sliced strawberries

1 can (20 ounces) crushed pineapple, undrained

1 package (about 16 ounces) angel food cake mix

1. Preheat oven to 350°F. Spray 13×9-inch baking pan with nonstick cooking spray.

2. Spread strawberries in prepared pan. Combine pineapple and cake mix in large bowl; beat 1 to 2 minutes or until well blended. Spread batter evenly over strawberries.

3. Bake 35 to 40 minutes or until toothpick inserted into center comes out clean. Cool 30 minutes before serving.

*Makes 12 to 15 servings*

# Peach Melba Dump Cake

2 cans (21 ounces each) peach pie filling

1 package (12 ounces) frozen raspberries, thawed and drained

1 package (about 15 ounces) yellow cake mix

½ cup (1 stick) butter, cut into thin slices

Ice cream (optional)

1. Preheat oven to 350°F. Spray 13×9-inch baking pan with nonstick cooking spray.

2. Spread peach pie filling in prepared pan; sprinkle with raspberries. Top evenly with cake mix. Top with butter in single layer, covering cake mix as much as possible.

3. Bake 40 to 45 minutes or until toothpick inserted into center of cake comes out clean. Cool at least 15 minutes before serving. Top with ice cream, if desired.

*Makes 12 to 15 servings*

# BLACKBERRY ALMOND DUMP CAKE

2 packages (12 ounces each) frozen blackberries, thawed and drained

¼ cup granulated sugar

1 package (about 15 ounces) yellow cake mix

¾ cup (1½ sticks) butter, cut into thin slices

½ cup sliced almonds

¼ cup packed brown sugar

1. Preheat oven to 350°F. Spray 13×9-inch baking pan with nonstick cooking spray.

2. Spread blackberries in prepared pan; sprinkle with granulated sugar and toss to coat. Top evenly with cake mix. Top with butter in single layer, covering cake mix as much as possible. Sprinkle with almonds and brown sugar.

3. Bake 50 to 60 minutes or until toothpick inserted into center of cake comes out clean. Cool at least 15 minutes before serving.

*Makes 12 to 15 servings*

# GRANOLA CARAMEL CARROT DUMP CAKE

1 can (20 ounces) crushed pineapple, undrained

1 package (about 15 ounces) carrot cake mix

½ cup (1 stick) butter, cut into thin slices

1 cup granola

3 tablespoons caramel topping, warmed

Ice cream (optional)

Sprigs fresh mint (optional)

1. Preheat oven to 350°F. Spray 13×9-inch baking pan with nonstick cooking spray.

2. Spread pineapple in prepared pan. Top evenly with cake mix. Top with butter in single layer, covering cake mix as much as possible. Sprinkle with granola; drizzle with caramel topping.

3. Bake 50 to 55 minutes or until toothpick inserted into center of cake comes out clean. Cool at least 15 minutes before serving. Top with ice cream, if desired. Garnish with mint.

*Makes 12 to 15 servings*

# Rainbow Dump Cake

1  can (20 ounces) crushed
   pineapple, undrained

1  can (14½ ounces) tart
   cherries in water, drained

1  package (about 15 ounces)
   yellow cake mix

½  cup (1 stick) butter, cut
   into thin slices

½  cup candy-coated
   chocolate pieces

1. Preheat oven to 350°F. Spray 13×9-inch baking pan with nonstick cooking spray.

2. Spread pineapple and cherries in prepared pan. Top evenly with cake mix. Top with butter in single layer, covering cake mix as much as possible.

3. Bake 35 to 40 minutes or until toothpick inserted into center of cake comes out clean, sprinkling with chocolate pieces during last 10 minutes of baking. Cool at least 15 minutes before serving.

*Makes 12 to 15 servings*

# Island Delight Dump Cake

3 ripe mangoes, peeled and cubed (about 4½ cups)

1 package (about 15 ounces) pineapple cake mix

1 can (12 ounces) lemon-lime or orange soda

½ cup chopped macadamia nuts (optional)

1. Preheat oven to 350°F. Spray 13×9-inch baking pan with nonstick cooking spray.

2. Spread mangoes in prepared pan. Top evenly with cake mix. Slowly pour soda over top, covering cake mix as much as possible. Sprinkle with macadamia nuts, if desired.

3. Bake 35 to 40 minutes or until toothpick inserted into center of cake comes out clean. Cool at least 15 minutes before serving.

*Makes 12 to 15 servings*

# MUG CAKES

# BERRY–PEACHY COBBLER

4 tablespoons plus
2 teaspoons sugar,
divided

¾ cup plus 2 tablespoons
all-purpose flour, divided

1¼ pounds peaches, peeled
and sliced *or* 1 package
(16 ounces) frozen
unsweetened sliced
peaches, thawed and
drained

2 cups fresh raspberries *or*
1 package (12 ounces)
frozen unsweetened
raspberries

1 teaspoon grated lemon
peel

½ teaspoon baking powder

½ teaspoon baking soda

⅛ teaspoon salt

2 tablespoons cold butter,
cut into small pieces

¼ cup plus 1 tablespoon
buttermilk

¼ cup plain Greek yogurt

1. Preheat oven to 425°F. Spray eight ramekins with nonstick cooking spray; place ramekins in jelly-roll pan.

2. Combine 2 tablespoons sugar and 2 tablespoons flour in large bowl. Add peaches, raspberries and lemon peel; toss to coat. Divide fruit evenly among prepared ramekins. Bake 15 minutes or until fruit is bubbly around edges.

3. Meanwhile, combine 2 tablespoons sugar, remaining ¾ cup flour, baking powder, baking soda and salt in medium bowl. Cut in butter with pastry blender or two knives until mixture resembles coarse crumbs. Stir in buttermilk and yogurt just until dry ingredients are moistened.

4. Remove ramekins from oven; top fruit with equal dollops of topping. Sprinkle topping with remaining 2 teaspoons sugar. Bake 18 to 20 minutes or until topping is lightly browned. Serve warm.

*Makes 8 servings*

# Mug-Made Mocha Cake

2 tablespoons whole
  wheat flour

2 tablespoons sugar

1 tablespoon cocoa powder,
  plus additional for
  garnish

1½ to 2 teaspoons instant
  coffee granules

1 egg white

3 tablespoons milk

1 teaspoon vegetable oil

2 teaspoons mini semisweet
  chocolate chips

1 tablespoon frozen
  whipped topping,
  thawed

## Microwave Directions

1. Combine flour, sugar, 1 tablespoon cocoa and coffee granules in large ceramic* microwavable mug; mix well. Whisk egg white, milk and oil in small bowl until well blended. Stir into flour mixture until smooth. Fold in chocolate chips.

2. Microwave on HIGH 2 minutes. Let stand 1 to 2 minutes before serving. Top with whipped topping and additional cocoa, if desired.

*Makes 1 serving*

*This cake will only work in a ceramic mug as the material allows for more even cooking than glass.

# NEON SPONGE CAKE TOWER

1 cup angel food cake mix

¾ cup water

Food coloring

Whipped topping

Colored sprinkles
(optional)

**Microwave Directions**

**1.** Combine ¼ cup cake mix and 3 tablespoons water in each of four 2-cup ramekins or small mugs. Add 3 to 5 drops desired food coloring to each to create desired color.

**2.** One at a time, microwave on HIGH 1½ minutes. Remove from microwave; let stand 10 minutes before removing from ramekins.

**3.** Remove cakes to plate. Cool completely.

**4.** Place 1 cake on serving plate. Top with whipped topping. Complete stack with remaining cakes and whipped topping. Top with sprinkles, if desired. Serve immediately.

*Makes 4 servings*

# CHOCOLATE AND PEANUT BUTTER MOLTEN CAKE

¼ cup all-purpose flour

1 tablespoon cocoa powder

2 tablespoons sugar

¼ teaspoon baking powder

¼ cup milk

2 tablespoons butter, melted

¼ teaspoon vanilla

1 teaspoon peanut butter

2 teaspoons mini semisweet chocolate chips, divided

*Microwave Directions*

1. Combine flour, cocoa, sugar and baking powder in medium bowl; mix well. Add milk, butter and vanilla; stirring until smooth. Pour batter into large microwavable mug or ramekin.

2. Place peanut butter and 1 teaspoon chocolate chips in center of batter; slightly press down.

3. Microwave on HIGH 1 minute. Remove from microwave; let stand 10 minutes.

4. Sprinkle with remaining 1 teaspoon chocolate chips.

*Makes 1 serving*

# PLUM–SIDE DOWN CAKES

2 tablespoons butter

3 tablespoons packed
   brown sugar

3 plums, sliced

½ cup granulated sugar

2 tablespoons shortening

1 egg

1 cup all-purpose flour

1 teaspoon baking powder

¼ teaspoon salt

⅓ cup milk

1. Preheat oven to 350°F. Spray eight standard (2½-inch) muffin cups with nonstick cooking spray.

2. Place butter in small microwavable bowl. Microwave on LOW (30%) just until melted. Stir in brown sugar. Spoon evenly into prepared muffin cups. Arrange plum slices in bottom of each cup.

3. Beat granulated sugar and shortening in medium bowl with electric mixer at medium speed until fluffy. Beat in egg until well combined. Combine flour, baking powder and salt in small bowl; beat into shortening mixture. Add milk; beat until smooth.

4. Spoon batter into prepared muffin cups, filling three fourths full. Place pan on baking sheet. Bake 20 to 22 minutes or until toothpick inserted into centers comes out clean.

5. Cool in pan 10 minutes. Run a knife around each cup. Invert onto wire rack; cool completely.

*Makes 8 cakes*

# Sinful Chocolate Mug Cake

¼ cup angel food cake mix

3 tablespoons water

2 teaspoons cocoa powder

Caramel sauce and chocolate syrup

Whipped topping (optional)

## Microwave Directions

1. Combine cake mix, water and cocoa in large (2-cup) microwavable mug; mix well.

2. Microwave on HIGH 1½ minutes. Remove from microwave; let stand 10 minutes.

3. Remove cake to plate. Drizzle with caramel sauce, chocolate syrup and top with whipped topping, if desired. Serve immediately.

*Makes 1 serving*

# PUMPKIN SPICE MUG CAKE

¼ cup angel food cake mix

3 tablespoons water

2 teaspoons solid-pack pumpkin

1 teaspoon finely chopped pecans

¼ teaspoon pumpkin pie spice

Whipped topping (optional)

Cinnamon and sugar (optional)

## Microwave Directions

1. Combine cake mix, water, pumpkin, pecans and pumpkin pie spice in large ceramic* microwavable mug; mix well.

2. Microwave on HIGH 2 minutes. Let stand 1 to 2 minutes before serving. Top with whipped topping, if desired. Sprinkle with cinnamon and sugar, if desired.

*Makes 1 serving*

*This cake will only work in a ceramic mug as the material allows for more even cooking than glass.

# PEPPERMINT-CHIP CAKE IN A CUP

¼ cup angel food cake mix

3 tablespoons water

1 tablespoon mini semisweet chocolate chips, plus additional for garnish

2 tablespoons frozen whipped topping, thawed

⅛ teaspoon peppermint extract

Crushed peppermints* (optional)

*To crush peppermints, place unwrapped candy in a heavy-duty resealable food storage bag. Loosely seal the bag, leaving an opening for air to escape. Crush the candies thoroughly with a rolling pin, meat mallet or the bottom of a heavy skillet.

## Microwave Directions

1. Combine cake mix, water and 1 tablespoon chocolate chips in large ceramic** microwavable mug.

2. Microwave on HIGH 1½ minutes. Let stand 1 to 2 minutes.

3. Meanwhile, stir whipped topping and peppermint extract in small bowl until well blended. Spoon over cake. Top with additional chocolate chips and crushed peppermints, if desired. Serve immediately.

*Makes 1 serving*

**This cake will only work in a ceramic mug as the material allows for more even cooking than glass.

# RED VELVET MUG CAKES

PAM® Original No-Stick Cooking Spray

5 seconds REDDI-WIP® Original Dairy Whipped Topping (about 2 cups)

¼ cup EGG BEATERS® Original

½ cup dry red velvet cake mix

3 tablespoons cream cheese spread

2 servings REDDI-WIP® Original Dairy Whipped Topping

1 tablespoon granulated sugar

## For cakes

1. Spray insides of 2 large microwave-safe mugs with cooking spray. Whisk together 5 seconds REDDI-WIP, EGG BEATERS and cake mix in medium bowl. Place half of batter in each mug. Microwave each mug individually on HIGH 1 minute to 1 minute 15 seconds or until set.

## For frosting

2. Stir together cream cheese spread, 2 servings REDDI-WIP and sugar in small bowl until blended. Invert each cake onto a plate; top each with half of the frosting.

*Makes 2 servings*

# CARROT CUP CAKE

5 tablespoons all-purpose flour

2 tablespoons granulated sugar

1 tablespoon packed brown sugar

1 tablespoon baking powder

½ teaspoon ground cinnamon

⅛ teaspoon salt

2 tablespoons grated carrot

2 tablespoons canola oil

1 egg

2 tablespoons shredded coconut

1 tablespoon walnuts

1 tablespoon currants

¼ cup powdered sugar

1 to 2 teaspoons milk

1. Adjust oven rack to center position. Preheat oven to 350°F. Spray inside of 6-ounce mug with nonstick cooking spray.

2. Combine flour, granulated sugar, brown sugar, baking powder, cinnamon and salt in small bowl; mix well. Add carrot, oil and egg; mix well. Add coconut, walnuts and currants; stir until well blended. Pour into prepared mug.

3. Bake 25 minutes or until toothpick inserted into center comes out clean. Combine powdered sugar and milk in small bowl; drizzle glaze over cake.

*Makes 1 serving*

# EVERYDAY CAKES

# St. Louis Gooey Butter Cake

1 package (about 15 ounces) yellow cake mix *without* pudding in the mix

½ cup (1 stick) butter, melted

4 eggs, divided

1 package (8 ounces) cream cheese, softened

1 teaspoon vanilla

3 cups powdered sugar, plus additional for topping

1. Preheat oven to 350°F. Spray 13×9-inch baking pan with nonstick cooking spray.

2. Beat cake mix, butter and 2 eggs in large bowl with electric mixer at low speed 1 minute or just until blended. Press mixture evenly onto bottom of prepared pan.

3. Beat cream cheese, remaining 2 eggs and vanilla in medium bowl with electric mixer at medium-high speed 1 minute or until well blended. Slowly add 3 cups powdered sugar; beat until smooth. Spread evenly over cake mix layer in pan.

4. Bake 35 to 40 minutes or until top is lightly browned. (Cake will puff up then collapse during baking to make gooey center.) Cool completely in pan on wire rack. Sprinkle with additional powdered sugar, if desired.

*Makes 12 to 15 servings*

# SNACKING APPLESAUCE CAKE SQUARES

⅓ cup butter, softened

2 eggs

⅔ cup thawed frozen unsweetened apple juice concentrate

½ cup unsweetened applesauce

2 cups all-purpose flour

2 teaspoons baking powder

2 teaspoons ground cinnamon, plus additional for topping

½ teaspoon baking soda

¼ teaspoon salt

1 large cooking apple, peeled and chopped

Whipped topping (optional)

1. Preheat oven to 375°F. Grease 9-inch square baking pan.

2. Beat butter in large bowl with electric mixter at medium speed until creamy. Blend in eggs, apple juice concentrate and applesauce. Combine flour, baking powder, 2 teaspoons cinnamon, baking soda and salt in separate large bowl. Gradually add to egg mixture, beating until well blended. Stir in apple. Spread batter evenly into prepared pan.

3. Bake 20 to 25 minutes or until toothpick inserted into center comes out clean. Cool on wire rack. Cut into squares. Top with whipped topping and additional cinnamon, if desired.

*Makes 9 servings*

# CHOCOLATE CRISPY TREAT CAKE

1 package (about 15 ounces) chocolate fudge cake mix, plus ingredients to prepare mix

1 cup semisweet chocolate chips

¼ cup light corn syrup

¼ cup (½ stick) butter

½ cup powdered sugar

2 cups crisp rice cereal

4 cups mini marshmallows (half of 10½-ounce package)

1. Preheat oven to 350°F. Grease bottom of 13×9-inch baking pan. Prepare cake mix according to package directions; pour into prepared pan. Bake 28 minutes or until toothpick inserted into center comes out almost clean.

2. Meanwhile, heat chocolate chips, corn syrup and butter in large saucepan over low heat, stirring frequently, until chocolate and butter are melted. Remove from heat; stir in powdered sugar. Gently stir in cereal until well blended.

3. Sprinkle marshmallows over top of cake. Bake 2 to 3 minutes or until marshmallows puff up slightly.

4. Spread chocolate cereal mixture over marshmallows. Let stand until set.

*Makes 12 to 15 servings*

NOTE: This cake is best eaten within a day or two of baking. The cereal will become soggy if the cake sits any longer.

# Sweet and Sour Brunch Cake

1 package (16 ounces) frozen rhubarb, thawed and patted dry*

1 cup packed brown sugar

1 tablespoon all-purpose flour

1 teaspoon ground cinnamon

¼ cup (½ stick) butter, cut into small pieces

1 package (about 15 ounces) yellow cake mix *without* pudding in the mix

1 package (4-serving size) vanilla instant pudding and pie filling mix

4 eggs

⅔ cup sour cream

½ cup water

½ cup vegetable oil

*If frozen rhubarb is unavailable, you may substitute frozen unsweetened strawberries.

1. Preheat oven to 350°F. Spray 13×9-inch baking pan with nonstick cooking spray.

2. Spread rhubarb evenly in single layer in prepared baking pan. Combine brown sugar, flour and cinnamon in small bowl; mix well. Sprinkle evenly over rhubarb; dot with butter.

3. Beat cake mix, pudding mix, eggs, sour cream, water and oil in large bowl with electric mixer at low speed 1 minute. Beat at medium speed 2 minutes or until well blended. Spread over rhubarb mixture.

4. Bake 40 minutes or until toothpick inserted into center comes out clean. Cool in pan 5 minutes. Invert onto serving plate.

*Makes 12 to 15 servings*

# TOFFEE SNACK CAKE

1½ cups all-purpose flour

1¼ cups chocolate-covered toffee bits

1 cup packed dark brown sugar

¾ cup chopped pecans, toasted*

1 teaspoon baking soda

¼ teaspoon salt

1 cup half-and-half

6 tablespoons (¾ stick) butter, melted and cooled

1 tablespoon white vinegar

1 teaspoon vanilla

*To toast pecans, spread in single layer in small heavy skillet. Cook over medium heat 1 to 2 minutes, stirring frequently, or until lightly browned. Remove from skillet immediately.

1. Preheat oven to 350°F. Coat 9-inch square baking pan with nonstick cooking spray.

2. Combine flour, toffee bits, brown sugar, pecans, baking soda and salt in large bowl; stir well.

3. Combine half-and-half, butter, vinegar and vanilla in medium bowl; stir well. Add half-and-half mixture to dry ingredients; mix well. Pour batter into prepared pan.

4. Bake 32 to 35 minutes or until toothpick inserted into center comes out clean.

*Makes 9 servings*

NOTE: Toffee Snack Cake tastes best on the day it's baked. To retain flavor, freeze any leftovers in an airtight container.

# PB&J Cookie Bars

1 package (about 15 ounces) yellow cake mix with pudding in the mix

1 cup peanut butter

½ cup vegetable oil

2 eggs

1 cup strawberry jam

1 cup peanut butter chips

1. Preheat oven to 350°F. Line 15×10-inch jelly-roll pan with foil and spray with nonstick cooking spray.

2. Beat cake mix, peanut butter, oil and eggs in large bowl with electric mixer at medium speed until well blended. With damp hands, press mixture evenly into bottom of prepared pan. Bake 20 minutes; cool in pan on wire rack.

3. Place jam in small microwavable bowl. Microwave on HIGH 20 seconds to soften. Spread jam evenly over cookie base. Sprinkle peanut butter chips over top.

4. Bake 10 minutes or until edges are browned. Cool completely in pan on wire rack. Remove foil; cut into bars.

*Makes about 3 dozen*

# BLUEBERRY SNACK CAKE

¾ cup all-purpose flour

¾ cup whole wheat flour

1 teaspoon baking soda

½ teaspoon ground
   cinnamon

¼ teaspoon salt

1 cup packed light brown
   sugar

6 tablespoons (¾ cup)
   butter, melted and
   cooled

1 tablespoon white vinegar

1 teaspoon vanilla

1¼ cups sour cream

1 cup toasted sweetened
   shredded coconut*

¾ cup dried blueberries

*To toast coconut, spread on
baking sheet. Toast 2 minutes in
preheated 350°F oven. Remove
from oven immediately.

1. Preheat oven to 350°F. Spray 9-inch
square baking pan with nonstick cooking
spray. Combine all-purpose flour, whole
wheat flour, baking soda, cinnamon and salt
in medium bowl.

2. Combine brown sugar, butter, vinegar
and vanilla in large bowl; mix well. Add
flour mixture and sour cream; mix well. Stir
in coconut and blueberries. Spread batter
in prepared pan.

3. Bake 35 minutes or until toothpick
inserted into center comes out clean. Cool
completely in pan on wire rack.

*Makes 9 servings*

# BROWNIE ICE CREAM TREATS

½ cup all-purpose flour

½ teaspoon salt

¼ teaspoon baking powder

6 tablespoons (¾ stick) butter

1 cup sugar

½ cup unsweetened Dutch process cocoa powder

2 eggs

½ teaspoon vanilla

8 (2¼-inch) jars with lids

2 cups pistachio or any flavor ice cream, slightly softened

Hot fudge topping, heated (optional)

1. Preheat oven to 350°F. Spray 9-inch square baking pan with nonstick cooking spray. Combine flour, salt and baking powder in small bowl.

2. Melt butter in medium saucepan over low heat. Stir in sugar until blended. Stir in cocoa until well blended. Stir in eggs, one at a time, then vanilla. Stir in flour mixture until blended. Pour into prepared pan.

3. Bake 20 minutes or until toothpick inserted into center comes out with fudgy crumbs. Cool completely in pan on wire rack.

4. For jars, cut out 16 brownies using 2-inch round cookie or biscuit cutter. (See Tip.) Remove brownie scraps from pan (any pieces left between round cut-outs); crumble into small pieces. Save remaining brownies for another use.

5. Place one brownie in each of eight ½-cup glass jars. Top with 2 tablespoons ice cream, pressing to form flat layer over brownie. Repeat brownie and ice cream layers.

6. Drizzle with hot fudge topping, if desired, and sprinkle with brownie crumbs. Serve immediately or make ahead through step 5. Cover and freeze until ready to serve.

*Makes 8 servings*

TIP: Measure the diameter of your jar first and cut out your brownies slightly smaller to fit in the jar. If your jar is not tall enough to fit two brownie layers, cut the brownies in half horizontally with a serrated knife.

# Lazy-Daisy Cake

2 cups granulated sugar

4 eggs

8 tablespoons (1 stick) butter, softened and divided

2 teaspoons vanilla

2 cups all-purpose flour

2 teaspoons baking powder

1 cup warm milk

1 cup flaked coconut

½ cup plus 2 tablespoons packed brown sugar

⅓ cup half-and-half

1. Preheat oven to 350°F. Grease 13×9-inch baking pan.

2. Beat granulated sugar, eggs, 4 tablespoons butter and vanilla in large bowl with electric mixer at medium speed 3 minutes or until fluffy. Sift flour and baking powder into medium bowl. Beat into egg mixture until well blended. Stir in milk. Pour batter into prepared pan. Bake 30 minutes or until toothpick inserted into center comes out clean.

3. Meanwhile, combine remaining 4 tablespoons butter, coconut, brown sugar and half-and-half in medium saucepan over medium heat. Cook until sugar is dissolved and butter is melted, stirring constantly.

4. Spread coconut mixture over warm cake. *Turn oven to broil.* Broil 4 inches from heat source 2 to 3 minutes or until top is light golden brown.

*Makes 12 to 15 servings*

# CHOCOLATE MYSTERY CAKE

1 package (about 15 ounces) German chocolate cake mix

1½ cups plus 2 tablespoons root beer (not diet soda), divided

2 eggs

¼ cup vegetable oil

1 container (about 16 ounces) vanilla frosting

1. Preheat oven to 350°F. Coat 13×9-inch baking pan with nonstick cooking spray.

2. Combine cake mix, 1½ cups root beer, eggs and oil in large bowl. Beat with electric mixer at low speed 30 seconds. Beat at medium speed 2 minutes or until well blended. Spread batter in prepared pan.

3. Bake 30 minutes or until toothpick inserted into center comes out clean. Cool completely in pan on wire rack.

4. Beat frosting and remaining 2 tablespoons root beer in medium bowl with electric mixer at medium speed 2 minutes or until fluffy. Frost top of cooled cake.

*Makes 12 to 15 servings*

# CARROT SNACK CAKE

1 package (about 15 ounces) butter recipe yellow cake mix with pudding in the mix, plus ingredients to prepare mix

2 jars (4 ounces each) strained carrot baby food

1½ cups chopped walnuts, divided

1 cup shredded carrots

½ cup golden raisins

1½ teaspoons ground cinnamon

1½ teaspoons vanilla, divided

1 package (8 ounces) cream cheese, softened

Grated peel of 1 lemon

2 teaspoons lemon juice

3 cups powdered sugar

1. Preheat oven to 350°F. Grease 13×9-inch baking pan.

2. Prepare cake mix according to package directions, using ½ cup water instead of amount called for in directions. Stir carrot baby food, 1 cup walnuts, carrots, raisins, cinnamon and ½ teaspoon vanilla into batter. Spread in prepared pan.

3. Bake 40 minutes or until toothpick inserted into center comes out clean. Cool completely in pan on wire rack.

4. Beat cream cheese in large bowl with electric mixer at medium speed until fluffy. Beat in lemon peel, lemon juice and remaining 1 teaspoon vanilla. Gradually add powdered sugar; beat until well blended and smooth. Spread frosting over cake; sprinkle with remaining ½ cup walnuts. Refrigerate 2 hours before serving.

*Makes 12 to 15 servings*

# BANANA SPLIT ICE CREAM CAKE

1 package (about 16 ounces) refrigerated chocolate chip cookie dough

2 ripe bananas, mashed

½ cup strawberry jam

4 cups strawberry ice cream, softened

  Hot fudge topping

  Whipped cream

12 to 15 maraschino cherries

1. Let dough stand at room temperature about 15 minutes. Preheat oven to 350°F. Lightly grease 13×9-inch baking pan.

2. Beat dough and bananas in large bowl with electric mixer at medium speed until well blended. Spread dough evenly in prepared pan and smooth top. Bake 22 minutes or until edges are light brown. Cool completely in pan on wire rack.

3. Line 8-inch square baking pan with foil or plastic wrap, allowing some to hang over edges of pan. Remove cooled cookie from pan; cut in half crosswise. Place 1 cookie half, top side down, in 8-inch pan, trimming edges to fit, if necessary. Spread ¼ cup jam evenly over cookie. Spread ice cream evenly over jam. Spread remaining ¼ cup jam over bottom of remaining cookie half; place jam side down over ice cream. Wrap tightly with foil; freeze at least 2 hours or overnight.

4. Cut into bars and top with hot fudge topping, whipped cream and cherries.

*Makes 12 to 15 servings*

# PEANUT CRUMB CAKE

1 package (about 15 ounces) yellow cake mix

¾ cup peanut butter

¼ cup packed brown sugar

1 cup water

3 eggs

¼ cup vegetable oil

⅓ cup mini semisweet chocolate chips

¼ cup peanut butter chips

¼ cup roasted peanuts, finely chopped

1. Preheat oven to 350°F. Lightly spray 13×9-inch baking pan with nonstick cooking spray.

2. Beat cake mix, peanut butter and brown sugar in large bowl with electric mixer at low speed until mixture resembles coarse crumbs. Remove ⅓ cup to medium bowl for topping. Add water, eggs and oil to remaining mixture; beat at medium speed until well blended.

3. Spread batter evenly in prepared pan. Add chocolate chips, peanut butter chips and peanuts to reserved crumb mixture; mix well. Sprinkle over batter.

4. Bake 38 to 42 minutes or until toothpick inserted into center comes out clean. Cool cake completely in pan on wire rack.

*Makes 12 to 15 servings*

# Luscious Lime Angel Food Cake Rolls

1 package (about 16 ounces) angel food cake mix

2 to 4 drops green food coloring (optional)

2 containers (8 ounces each) lime-flavored yogurt

Lime slices (optional)

1. Preheat oven to 350°F. Line two 17×11-inch jelly-roll pans with parchment or waxed paper; set aside.

2. Prepare angel food cake mix according to package directions. Divide batter evenly between prepared pans. Draw knife through batter to remove large air bubbles. Bake 12 minutes or until cakes are lightly browned and toothpick inserted into centers comes out clean.

3. Invert each cake onto separate clean towel. Starting at short end, roll up warm cake jelly-roll fashion, with towel inside. Cool cakes completely.

4. Place 1 to 2 drops green food coloring in each container of yogurt, if desired; stir well. Unroll cakes; remove towels. Spread each cake with 1 container yogurt, leaving 1-inch border. Roll up cakes; place seam side down. Slice each cake roll into eight pieces. Garnish with lime slices, if desired. Serve immediately or refrigerate.

*Makes 16 servings*

# Frosted Spiced Sweet Potato Cake

1½ pounds sweet potato
   (1 very large or
   2 medium), cut in half
   lengthwise and crosswise

1½ cups all-purpose flour

1¼ cups granulated sugar

2 teaspoons baking powder

1 teaspoon ground
   cinnamon

½ teaspoon baking soda

½ teaspoon salt

¼ teaspoon ground allspice

¾ cup canola oil

2 eggs

½ cup chopped walnuts or
   pecans, plus additional
   for garnish

½ cup raisins

1 container (16 ounces)
   cream cheese frosting

1. Place sweet potato in large saucepan with 1 inch water. Cover and cook over medium heat 30 minutes or until fork-tender, adding additional water during cooking, if necessary. Drain potato; peel and mash when cool enough to handle. (You should have 2 cups.)

2. Preheat oven to 325°F. Spray 13×9-inch baking pan with nonstick cooking spray.

3. Combine flour, granulated sugar, baking powder, cinnamon, baking soda, salt and allspice in medium bowl. Beat sweet potatoes, oil and eggs in large bowl with electric mixer at low speed until blended. Add flour mixture; beat at medium speed 30 seconds or until well blended, scraping down bowl occasionally. Stir in ½ cup walnuts and raisins. Spoon batter into prepared pan.

4. Bake 35 minutes or until toothpick inserted into center comes out clean. Cool completely in pan on wire rack.

5. Spread frosting over cake; sprinkle with additional walnuts. Store cake, covered, in refrigerator.

*Makes 12 to 15 servings*

# CHOCOLATE YOGURT CAKE

⅔ cup plus 2 tablespoons unsweetened Dutch process cocoa powder, divided

1¾ cups all-purpose flour

2 teaspoons baking powder

1 teaspoon salt

½ teaspoon baking soda

2 cups (16 ounces) whole-milk plain yogurt, divided

⅓ cup water

1 teaspoon vanilla

1¼ cups granulated sugar

6 tablespoons (¾ stick) butter, softened

2 eggs

1 cup semisweet chocolate chips

½ cup powdered sugar, sifted

1. Preheat oven to 350°F. Spray 13×9-inch baking pan with nonstick cooking spray. Dust with 2 tablespoons cocoa powder; tap out excess.

2. Combine remaining ⅔ cup cocoa, flour, baking powder, salt and baking soda in medium bowl. Whisk 1 cup yogurt, water and vanilla in small bowl until well blended.

3. Beat granulated sugar and butter in large bowl with electric mixer at medium speed 1 minute or until light and fluffy. Add eggs; beat 1 minute. Gradually add flour mixture; beat at low speed just until combined. Add yogurt mixture; beat 1 minute, scraping down side of bowl once. Pour batter into prepared pan.

4. Bake 35 to 40 minutes or until toothpick inserted into center comes out clean. Cool cake completely in pan on wire rack.

5. Meanwhile, for frosting, place chocolate chips and remaining 1 cup yogurt in medium microwavable bowl. Microwave on HIGH 30 seconds; stir. Continue microwaving at 10-second intervals until chocolate is melted and mixture is smooth. Whisk in powdered sugar until well blended. Spread over cooled cake.

*Makes 12 to 15 servings*

# Heart-of-the-Home Orange Coffeecake

## COFFEECAKE

1½ cups all-purpose flour

1½ teaspoons baking powder

1 teaspoon baking soda

1 cup sugar

½ cup (1 stick) unsalted butter, softened

2 eggs

1 cup sour cream

1 teaspoon orange extract

## TOPPING

1 cup chopped walnuts

½ cup sugar

1 teaspoon ground cinnamon

½ teaspoon ground nutmeg

1. Preheat oven to 350°F. Spray 8- or 9-inch square pan with nonstick cooking spray.

2. For coffeecake, combine flour, baking powder and baking soda in medium bowl; mix well. Place 1 cup sugar and butter in large bowl; mix with electric mixer at medium speed until smooth. Add eggs, sour cream and orange extract; mix well. Add flour mixture one third at a time, mixing well after each addition.

3. For topping, combine walnuts, ½ cup sugar, cinnamon and nutmeg in small bowl; mix well. Add ½ cup topping mixture to batter; stir to combine. Pour batter into prepared pan. Sprinkle remaining topping mixture over batter.

4. Bake 40 to 50 minutes or until toothpick inserted into center comes out clean.

*Makes 8 to 9 servings*

# CUTE CUPCAKES

# ANGELIC CUPCAKES

1 package (about 16 ounces) angel food cake mix

1¼ cups cold water

¼ teaspoon peppermint extract (optional)

Red food coloring

4½ cups light whipped topping

1. Preheat oven to 375°F. Line 36 standard (2½-inch) muffin cups with paper baking cups.

2. Beat cake mix, water and peppermint extract, if desired, in large bowl with electric mixer at low speed 2 minutes. Pour half of batter into medium bowl; fold in 9 drops red food coloring. Alternate spoonfuls of white and pink batter in each prepared muffin cup, filling three fourths full.

3. Bake 11 minutes or until cupcakes are golden brown with deep cracks on top. Cool in pans 10 minutes. Remove to wire racks; cool completely.

4. Divide whipped topping between two small bowls. Add 2 drops red food coloring to one bowl; stir gently until whipped topping is evenly colored. Frost cupcakes with pink and white whipped topping as desired.

*Makes 36 cupcakes*

# Marshmallow Fudge Sundae Cupcakes

1 package (about 15 ounces) chocolate cake mix, plus ingredients to prepare mix

2 packages (4 ounces each) waffle bowls

40 large marshmallows

1 jar (8 ounces) hot fudge topping

Colored sprinkles or chopped nuts

1¼ cups whipped topping

1 jar (10 ounces) maraschino cherries

1. Preheat oven to 350°F. Lightly spray 20 standard (2½-inch) muffin cups with nonstick cooking spray.

2. Prepare cake mix according to package directions. Spoon batter into prepared muffin cups, filling two thirds full.

3. Bake 20 minutes or until toothpick inserted into centers comes out clean. Cool in pans 10 minutes. Remove to wire racks; cool completely.

4. Place waffle bowls on ungreased baking sheets. Place one cupcake in each waffle bowl. Top each cupcake with 2 marshmallows; return to oven 2 minutes or until marshmallows are slightly softened.

5. Remove lid from hot fudge topping; microwave on HIGH 10 seconds or until softened. Top each cupcake with hot fudge topping, sprinkles, whipped topping and cherry.

*Makes 20 cupcakes*

# Pineapple Upside-Down Cupcakes

1 can (20 ounces) pineapple
   chunks in syrup

1 cup packed brown sugar

1 package (about
   15 ounces) yellow cake
   mix, plus ingredients to
   prepare mix

12 maraschino cherries,
   halved

1. Preheat oven to 350°F. Spray 24 standard (2½-inch) muffin cups with nonstick cooking spray. Drain pineapple, reserving ¼ cup syrup.

2. Place 2 teaspoons brown sugar in each prepared muffin cup. Cut 2 pineapple chunks horizontally to create 4 wedge-shaped pieces. Arrange pineapple pieces over brown sugar to resemble flower petals.

3. Prepare cake mix according to package directions, substituting ¼ cup pineapple syrup for ¼ cup water called for in package directions. Spoon batter over pineapple in muffin cups, filling three fourths full.

4. Bake 20 minutes or until toothpick inserted into centers comes out clean. Cool in pans 10 minutes; invert pans onto serving plates. Place cherry half in center of each cupcake.

*Makes 24 cupcakes*

# Penguins Cupcakes

1 package (about 15 ounces) cake mix, any flavor, plus ingredients to prepare mix

Orange chewy fruit candy squares

1 container (16 ounces) white frosting

Black gel frosting*

*If black gel frosting is not available, you can tint white frosting with black food coloring. You'll need 1½ containers of white frosting for the recipe; use 1 container to coat the cupcakes with white frosting and tint the remaining ½ container with black food coloring. Or, you can use melted semisweet chocolate instead of black frosting to decorate the penguins.

1. Preheat oven to 350°F. Line 22 standard (2½-inch) muffin cups with paper baking cups. Prepare cake mix according to package directions. Spoon batter into prepared muffin cups, filling two thirds full.

2. Bake 20 minutes or until toothpick inserted into centers comes out clean. Cool in pans 10 minutes. Remove to wire racks; cool completely.

3. Working with one candy square at a time, unwrap candy and microwave on LOW (30%) 5 seconds or just until softened. Press candies between hands or on waxed paper to flatten to ⅛-inch thickness. Use scissors or paring knife to cut out feet and triangles for beaks.

4. Place white frosting in medium microwavable bowl; microwave on HIGH about 10 seconds until very soft but not completely melted. Dip tops of cupcakes into frosting to coat; let stand on wire racks until set.

5. Place black frosting in piping bag (or use can of frosting with piping tip); pipe outline of penguin around edge of each cupcake as shown in photo. Pipe eyes on cupcakes; press beaks and feet into frosting.

*Makes 22 cupcakes*

# COLA FLOAT CUPCAKES

1 package (about 15 ounces) vanilla cake mix, plus ingredients to prepare mix

1 can (12 ounces) cola beverage

Cola Buttercream (recipe follows)

Vanilla Buttercream (recipe follows)

Maraschino cherries

1. Prepare cake mix according to package directions, substituting cola for water.

2. Line 18 standard (2½-inch) muffin cups with paper baking cups. Pour batter evenly into prepared muffin cups and bake according to cupcake directions. Cool completely on wire rack.

3. Prepare Cola Buttercream and Vanilla Buttercream. Frost and garnish each cupcake with maraschino cherry.

*Makes 18 cupcakes*

**COLA BUTTERCREAM:** Beat ½ cup (1 stick) butter, softened, and 1½ cups powdered sugar in large bowl with electric mixer at medium speed until smooth. Stir in 2 tablespoons cola, adding additional in small drops, if necessary, until frosting is creamy and spreadable. Makes about 1 cup.

**VANILLA BUTTERCREAM:** Beat 5½ tablespoons butter, softened, and 2½ cups powdered sugar in large bowl with electric mixer at medium speed until smooth. Stir in 2 teaspoons vanilla and 1 tablespoon milk. Makes about 1 cup.

# POKED TURTLE CUPCAKES

1 package (about 15 ounces) chocolate cake mix, plus ingredients to prepare mix

24 whole pecans

24 caramels, unwrapped

1 container (16 ounces) chocolate frosting

2 cups chopped pecans

1. Prepare cake mix according to package directions. Line 24 standard (2½-inch) muffin cups with paper baking cups. Place whole pecan in bottom of each cup; fill three fourths full with batter. Bake according to package directions for cupcakes.

2. Poke hole in center of each cupcake with round wooden spoon handle. Place 1 unwrapped caramel in center of each cupcake. Frost cupcakes; sprinkle with chopped pecans.

*Makes 24 cupcakes*

# Koala Cupcakes

1 package (about 15 ounces) cake mix, any flavor, plus ingredients to prepare mix

1 container (16 ounces) white frosting

Black food coloring

White chocolate candy discs

Jumbo pink confetti sprinkles

Small round white candies

Black jelly beans or chocolate-covered raisins

Black decorating gel

1. Preheat oven to 350°F. Line 22 standard (2½-inch) muffin cups with paper baking cups. Prepare cake mix according to package directions. Spoon batter into prepared muffin cups, filling two thirds full.

2. Bake 20 minutes or until toothpick inserted into centers comes out clean. Cool in pans 10 minutes. Remove to wire racks; cool completely.

3. Place frosting in medium microwavable bowl. Add food coloring, a few drops at a time, until desired shade of gray is reached. Microwave on HIGH about 10 seconds or until very soft but not completely melted. Dip tops of cupcakes in frosting to coat; let stand on wire racks until set. Reserve remaining frosting.

4. Press candy discs into sides of cupcakes for ears; frost tops of discs. Place sprinkle in center of each disc. Attach white candies for eyes and jelly beans for noses. Pipe dot of decorating gel in each eye. Place reserved frosting in piping bag fitted with star tip; pipe frosting on tops of cupcakes to resemble fur.

*Makes 22 cupcakes*

# LEMON MERINGUE CUPCAKES

1 package (about 18 ounces) lemon cake mix, plus ingredients to prepare mix

¾ cup prepared lemon curd*

4 egg whites, at room temperature

6 tablespoons sugar

*Lemon curd, a thick sweet lemon spread, is available in many supermarkets near the jams and preserves.

1. Preheat oven to 350°F. Line 9 jumbo (3½-inch) muffin cups with paper baking cups. Prepare cake mix according to package directions. Spoon batter into prepared muffin cups, filling two thirds full.

2. Bake 20 to 25 minutes or until toothpick inserted into centers comes out clean. Cool in pans 10 minutes. Remove to wire racks; cool completely. *Increase oven temperature to 375°F.*

3. Cut off tops of cupcakes with serrated knife. (Do not remove paper baking cups.) Scoop out small hole in center of each cupcake with tablespoon; fill with generous tablespoon lemon curd. Replace cupcake tops.

4. Beat egg whites in medium bowl with electric mixer at high speed until soft peaks form. Gradually add sugar, beating until stiff peaks form. Pipe or spread meringue in peaks on each cupcake.

5. Place cupcakes on baking sheet. Bake 5 minutes or until peaks of meringue are golden.

*Makes 9 jumbo cupcakes*

VARIATION: This recipe can also be used to make 24 standard (2½-inch) cupcakes. Line muffin pans with paper baking cups. Prepare and bake cake mix according to package directions. Cut off tops of cupcakes; scoop out hole in each cupcake with teaspoon and fill with generous teaspoon lemon curd. Pipe or spread meringue in peaks on each cupcake; bake as directed above.

# Grape Soda Cupcakes

1½ cups all-purpose flour

1 (0.14-ounce) envelope grape unsweetened drink mix

2 teaspoons baking powder

⅛ teaspoon salt

1 cup granulated sugar

1 cup (2 sticks) unsalted butter, softened and divided

2 eggs

½ cup plus 3 tablespoons milk, divided

1½ teaspoons vanilla, divided

3 cups powdered sugar

Purple food coloring

White sugar pearls (optional)

1. Preheat oven to 350°F. Line 12 standard (2½-inch) muffin cups with paper baking cups.

2. Whisk flour, drink mix, baking powder and salt in small bowl. Beat granulated sugar and ½ cup butter in medium bowl with electric mixer at medium speed until creamy. Add eggs, one at a time, beating well after each addition. Add flour mixture; beat until blended. Add ½ cup milk and 1 teaspoon vanilla; beat until smooth. Spoon batter evenly into prepared muffin cups.

3. Bake 20 minutes or until toothpick inserted into centers comes out clean. Cool in pan 10 minutes. Remove to wire rack; cool completely.

4. Meanwhile, beat powdered sugar, remaining ½ cup butter, 3 tablespoons milk and ½ teaspoon vanilla in large bowl with electric mixer at medium speed until fluffy. Add food coloring, a few drops at a time, until desired shade of purple is reached.

5. Pipe or spread frosting on cupcakes. Top with sugar pearls, if desired.

*Makes 12 cupcakes*

# Ice Cream Cone Cupcakes

24 flat-bottomed ice cream cones

1 package (about 15 ounces) white cake mix, plus ingredients to prepare mix

2 tablespoons colored nonpareils

Prepared vanilla and chocolate frostings

Additional colored nonpareils and decors

1. Preheat oven to 350°F. Stand ice cream cones in 13×9-inch baking pan or muffin cups.

2. Prepare cake mix according to package directions; stir in nonpareils. Spoon batter evenly into cones.

3. Bake 20 minutes or until toothpick inserted into centers comes out clean. Remove to wire racks; cool completely.

4. Frost cupcakes and decorate as desired.

*Makes 24 cupcakes*

NOTE: These cupcakes are best served the day they are made.

# CHERRY CUPCAKES

1 package (about 18 ounces) chocolate cake mix

3 eggs

1⅓ cups water

½ cup vegetable oil

1 (21-ounce) can cherry pie filling

1 (16-ounce) can vanilla frosting

Prepare cake mix according to package directions, using eggs, water and oil. Spoon batter into 24 paper-lined muffin pan cups, filling two-thirds full.

Remove 24 cherries from cherry filling; set aside. Spoon generous teaspoon of remaining cherry filling onto center of each cupcake.

Bake in preheated 350°F oven 20 to 25 minutes. Cool in pans on wire racks 10 minutes. Remove from pans. Let cool completely. Frost cupcakes with vanilla frosting. Garnish cupcakes with reserved cherries.

*Makes 24 cupcakes*

*Favorite Recipe from*
**Cherry Marketing Institute**

# Ladybug Cupcakes

1 package (about 15 ounces) cake mix, any flavor, plus ingredients to prepare mix

1 container (16 ounces) white frosting

Red food coloring

Chocolate-covered mint candies, chocolate malt balls or other round chocolate candies

Black string licorice

Mini semisweet chocolate chips

White and black decorating icings

1. Preheat oven to 350°F. Line 22 standard (2½-inch) muffin cups with paper baking cups. Prepare cake mix according to package directions. Spoon batter into prepared muffin cups, filling two thirds full.

2. Bake 20 minutes or until toothpick inserted into centers comes out clean. Cool in pans 10 minutes. Remove to wire racks; cool completely.

3. Place frosting in medium microwavable bowl. Add food coloring, a few drops at a time, until desired shade of red is reached. Microwave on HIGH about 10 seconds or until very soft but not completely melted. Dip tops of cupcakes in frosting to coat; let stand on wire racks until set.

4. Press chocolate candy into one side of each cupcake for head. Cut licorice into 2½-inch lengths; press into center of each cupcake running from head to opposite side. Arrange chocolate chips, point ends down, all over each cupcake. Pipe eyes and mouths with decorating icings.

*Makes 22 cupcakes*

TIP: To get the ladybug spots to lay flat, cut the pointed tips off the chocolate chips with a small paring knife.

# Index

# Acknowledgments

The publisher would like to thank the company and organization listed below
for the use of their recipes and photograph in this publication.

Cherry Marketing Institute
ConAgra Foods, Inc.

# METRIC CONVERSION CHART

## VOLUME MEASUREMENTS (dry)

1/8 teaspoon = 0.5 mL
1/4 teaspoon = 1 mL
1/2 teaspoon = 2 mL
3/4 teaspoon = 4 mL
1 teaspoon = 5 mL
1 tablespoon = 15 mL
2 tablespoons = 30 mL
1/4 cup = 60 mL
1/3 cup = 75 mL
1/2 cup = 125 mL
2/3 cup = 150 mL
3/4 cup = 175 mL
1 cup = 250 mL
2 cups = 1 pint = 500 mL
3 cups = 750 mL
4 cups = 1 quart = 1 L

## VOLUME MEASUREMENTS (fluid)

1 fluid ounce (2 tablespoons) = 30 mL
4 fluid ounces (1/2 cup) = 125 mL
8 fluid ounces (1 cup) = 250 mL
12 fluid ounces (1 1/2 cups) = 375 mL
16 fluid ounces (2 cups) = 500 mL

## WEIGHTS (mass)

1/2 ounce = 15 g
1 ounce = 30 g
3 ounces = 90 g
4 ounces = 120 g
8 ounces = 225 g
10 ounces = 285 g
12 ounces = 360 g
16 ounces = 1 pound = 450 g

## DIMENSIONS

1/16 inch = 2 mm
1/8 inch = 3 mm
1/4 inch = 6 mm
1/2 inch = 1.5 cm
3/4 inch = 2 cm
1 inch = 2.5 cm

## OVEN TEMPERATURES

250°F = 120°C
275°F = 140°C
300°F = 150°C
325°F = 160°C
350°F = 180°C
375°F = 190°C
400°F = 200°C
425°F = 220°C
450°F = 230°C

## BAKING PAN SIZES

| Utensil | Size in Inches/Quarts | Metric Volume | Size in Centimeters |
|---|---|---|---|
| Baking or Cake Pan (square or rectangular) | 8×8×2 | 2 L | 20×20×5 |
| | 9×9×2 | 2.5 L | 23×23×5 |
| | 12×8×2 | 3 L | 30×20×5 |
| | 13×9×2 | 3.5 L | 33×23×5 |
| Loaf Pan | 8×4×3 | 1.5 L | 20×10×7 |
| | 9×5×3 | 2 L | 23×13×7 |
| Round Layer Cake Pan | 8×1½ | 1.2 L | 20×4 |
| | 9×1½ | 1.5 L | 23×4 |
| Pie Plate | 8×1¼ | 750 mL | 20×3 |
| | 9×1¼ | 1 L | 23×3 |
| Baking Dish or Casserole | 1 quart | 1 L | — |
| | 1½ quart | 1.5 L | — |
| | 2 quart | 2 L | — |